1ST GRADE AMERICAN HISTORY
EARLY PILGRIMS OF AMERICA

Speedy Publishing LLC
40 E. Main St. #1156
Newark, DE 19711
www.speedypublishing.com

A Pilgrim is someone who travels for religious reasons.

The Pilgrims were a group
of English settlers who
left Europe in search
of religious freedom
in the Americas. They
founded the Plymouth
Colony in 1620.

The Pilgrims left because they were tired of the Government telling them what to believe and how to live.

They were called
"Separatists" because
they wanted to separate
from the Church of
England and worship
God in their own way.

The Pilgrims left for the New World on August 15, 1620. The Pilgrims originally set sail with two ships; the Speedwell and the Mayflower.

The Speedwell started to leak and had to return to port. The Mayflower managed to fit 102 total passengers.

The Pilgrims were finally successful in sailing on September 16, 1620.

The voyage across the Atlantic Ocean was long and difficult. They ran out of fresh water and many people became sick.

The Pilgrims didn't reach the new world until November 9, 1620.

The Pilgrims signed
a document that
is today called the
Mayflower Compact.

The compact declared that the colonists were loyal to the King of England, that they were Christians who served God, that they would make fair and just laws, and that they would each work for the good of the colony.

The Pilgrims searched for a good place to build a settlement. They eventually found a location called Plymouth.

By the fall of 1621, only half of the pilgrims survived. The survivors, thankful to be alive, decided to prepare a thanksgiving feast.

In the Pilgrim household,
the adults sat down to
dinner and the children
waited on them.

The first Thanksgiving celebration in the fall of 1621 went on for three days.